Dear Surabhi,

Happy reading!

♡
Garima !

Introduction to Biology
Cells

Contents

1 Difference Between Living and Non-living Things

1 Difference between living and non-living things

We are **surrounded** by **living** things such as plants and animals and **non-living** things such as books, stones, buildings etc.

Figure 1.a: Non-living and living things

Have you ever wondered what's the difference between a living and a non-living thing?
We know some characteristics of living things because we know that birds fly, dogs run, plants grow and produce fruits and vegetables.

If we throw a stone in the air, it can go flying. Shouldn't that make it a living thing? Similarly, water can convert into ice crystals and grow in size when the weather is very cold so does that make it a living thing?

The answer is No.

Neither the stone nor the ice crystals are living things.

There are seven characteristics of living things.

1. They eat: All living things consume some sort of source of energy from their environment to obtain energy for their growth. For example humans eat a variety of food products to keep themselves healthy.

2. They move: All living organisms show movement of one kind or another. Animals and humans show different types of external movements such as swimming, walking, running etc. Plants might not be able to move from one spot to another like we do, but they have the ability to move substances from one part of their body to another.

3. They breathe: All living things exchange gases with their environment. Animals take in oxygen and breathe out carbon dioxide. Plants take in carbon dioxide and breathe out oxygen.

4. They excrete (poop): As living bodies process food, waste products are generated that need to be removed from their bodies. This is called excretion. If this waste was allowed to remain in the body it could be poisonous. Humans produce a liquid waste called urine. We also excrete waste when we breathe out.

5. They grow: When living things feed they gain energy. Some of this energy is used in growth. Living things become larger and more complicated as they grow.

6. They respond to changes in their environment: We respond when things change around us such as light, heat, cold and sound, as do other living things. For example, if you are really cold, you might get goosebumps or even start to shiver.

7. They give birth to more of their kind: All living things produce young. Humans make babies, cats produce kittens and pigeons lay eggs. Plants also reproduce. Many make seeds which can germinate and grow into new plants.

Some non-living things may show one or two of these characteristics but living things show all seven characteristics.

Plants and animals are living things as they do all of those seven things.

Figure 1.b Examples of animal species

Figure 1.c Examples of plant species

Fun Fact

Scientists estimate that there are over 8.7 Million different types of animal species. Thats **8,700,000 types of animals!**
They also estimate that there are over **390,000 plant species** on earth

2

So What Makes Living Things... Living?

2 So what makes living things..Living?

We understand the differences between living and non-living things. Now, let's take a deeper look into living things.

If you look around yourself, you will notice a lot of variety amongst living things. Living things come in many shapes, sizes, colors, eating preferences and living environments.

For example, rabbits eat fruits and vegetables while lions eat meat. Elephants live on land while whales live in the oceans. Eagles can fly at great heights, armadillos live underground while snakes slither on the ground.

They also vary greatly in size.

The Blue whale is the largest animal on earth, reaching a weight of about **180 tons**.

That is about **100 times** the weight of an average **car**!

It's also about 98ft in length!.

The smallest animal on the earth is a tiny little frog.

This frog weighs less than **3 grams** and is only about **0.3 inches in length.**

Members of a particular species have similar features and behaviors but each species behaves differently than others. Each species has characteristics of its own.

For example, all **giraffes** have *spots and really long necks*. All **zebras have stripes and short necks**. Giraffes look *very different* than zebras.

Figure 2.b Differences between species

Similarly, plants also vary greatly in shapes, sizes, heights, weights and colors.

Plants have adapted to a variety of environments, from the desert to tropical rainforests to lakes and oceans. From tiny mosses to gorgeous rose bushes to extremely large redwood trees.

Figure 2.a Different types of plant shapes and sizes

A cactus is different from other plants because it grows in deserts where there isn't a lot of water. In order to preserve water, it has spines instead of leaves.

The flower with the world's largest bloom is the Rafflesia arnoldii. This rare flower is found in the rainforests of Indonesia. It can grow to be 3 feet across and weigh up to 15 pounds! It is a special type of plant - it's a parasite. It attaches itself to a host plant to obtain water and nutrients.

We humans are very different than other species on the earth. As of the writing of this book, there are over **7.34 Billion people on this earth!**

Every person in the world has the same features – *eyes, nose, arms, legs, and a face but every person looks different than the other.*

So what are all living things made of?
What makes them similar to others in their species and different from other species?

The answer lies in Cells!

We will learn more about the mystery of cells in the next chapter.

Fun Fact

Because cacti have to survive in harsh desert conditions where there is little water, they do everything they can to conserve the amount of water they have. A cactus plant holds its breath during the day and breathes in at night to conserve water.

3 What's a Cell?

3 What's a Cell?

In the previous chapter, we learned that all the great variety in living things can be attributed to cells. Despite the tremendous variety of life, the cells of all organisms are remarkably similar in composition and function. In fact chemically, they are virtually identical.

So if the cell makes up the blue whale, it must be really huge - Right?

But then, how does this giant cell fit inside the tiny little frog?

Actually, a cell is very, very, very small. A typical cell is only about **1/40th of a millimeter!**

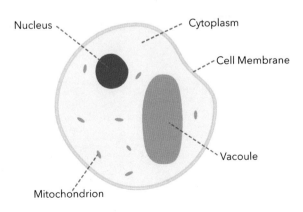

Figure 3.a Structure of a Cell

All living things are made up of tiny compartments called cells. A cell is a tiny bag of chemicals with a thin and flexible "skin" called a cell membrane.

A living organism might have one cell or trillions of cells.

3 What's a Cell?

There are many different types and number of cells that make up living things. That is how all the living things get their unique shape, size, variety and behavior.

The number of cells in different living things also vary dramatically.

  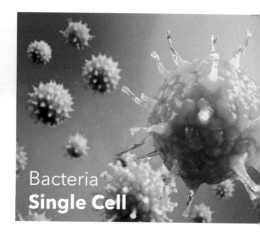

Figure 3.b Count of Cells in different organisms

Even though animals and plants have cells that perform different functions, all cells have three things in common.

Membrane: They have a skin called the cell membrane that encloses all the cell contents and separates it from the cell's environment. This "skin" keeps the contents of the cell together and controls the passage of nutrients into, and waste products out of the cell.

Cytoplasm: The bag is filled-up with a clear fluid called Cytoplasm (sy-toe-pla-zm). The cytoplasm is a jelly-like fluid found inside the cell and outside the nucleus. Various types of cell organs and minerals are suspended in this constantly streaming fluid. Apart from containing all the cell organelles, the cytoplasm also helps maintain the shape of a cell.

DNA: DNA is the short form of DeoxyriboNucleic Acid (dee-oxy-ry-bo-nu-cli-ek acid). I know -it's hard to pronounce. For now don't worry about spelling it out. Just know that DNA is one of the most important components of the cell since it contains all the genetic material which defines the purpose of the cell. DNA is so important for all living things that we will learn more about DNA in a later chapter.

All cells have the same basic chemical composition.

Fun Fact

When the baby starts to grow inside mommy's belly, it starts with just one cell. Later, when we are born and when we grow up, we have 37.2 trillion cells. Approximately 50 billion to 70 billion cells in a human body die every single day!

4 Types of Living Things

Based on these 3 components, there are TWO basic types of cells that make up all living things

1. **Prokaryotic** (*Pro-kary-otic*)
2. **Eukaryotic** (*U-kary-otic*)

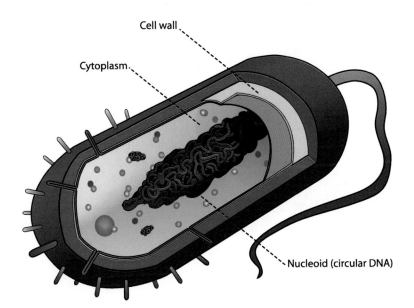

Prokaryotic organisms are made up of a single prokaryotic cell. These cells don't have a nucleus. These cells are smaller and simpler in structure.

Here is what this single cell looks likes.

Figure 4.a A Prokaryotic Cell

In addition, prokaryotic cells typically also have a tail that is used for movement. They also have fine hair on the surface. Since these cells don't have a nucleus, the single DNA molecule sits in the cytoplasm and forms a nucleoid.

An example of a Prokaryotic organism is **Bacteria**.

Eukaryotic organisms can have one or more cells. Eukaryotic cells are advanced and complex cells with membrane enclosed organelles. Organelles are tiny organs inside the cell, each one of which performs specific functions.

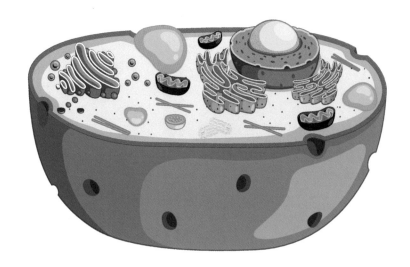

Figure 4.b A Eukaryotic Cell

Plants and animals are made up of Eukaryotic cells. Examples of eukaryotic cells are human brain cells and liver cells. These cells perform many different types of functions to enable the "life" of an organism. For example, the Red Blood Cells in the human body carry oxygen to different parts of the human body while the Bone cells make up and sustain our bones. We will learn more about this in a later chapter.

This function of the cell is defined by its DNA which is contained inside the nucleus. In order to understand how these different types of cells are created and how they operate together, lets learn more about the nucleus and the DNA it contains.

Stem Cells

Intestinal Cells

Blood Cells

Muscle Cells

LiverCells

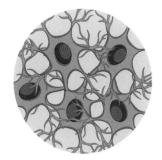

Brain Cells

Fun Fact

Did you know that our Earth is Four Billion, Five Hundred Forty Three Million years old. That's **4,543,000,000 YEARS**!! That's a lot of Zeros in any number…. Isn't it? The first living things on Earth emerged about 3.5 Billion years old. These are thought to have been single celled *prokaryotes*.

5 The Nucleus

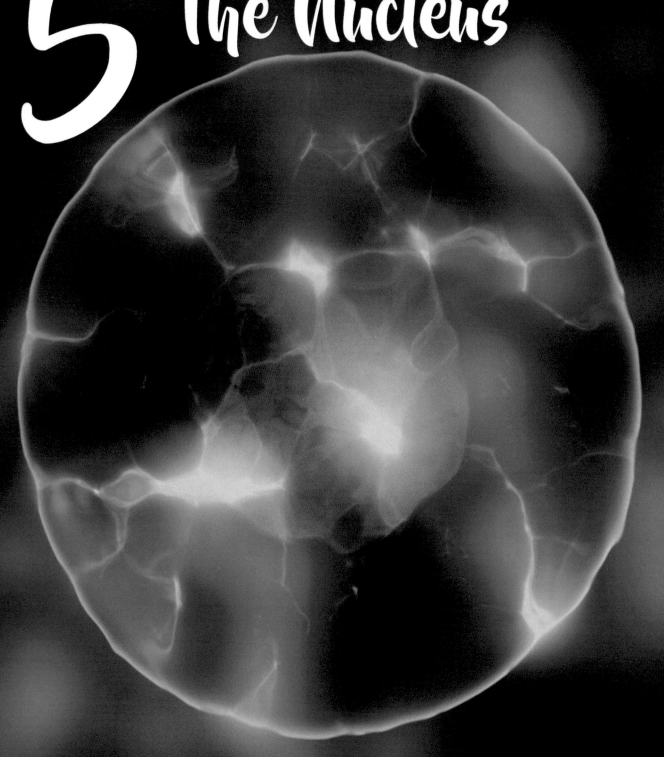

5 The Nucleus

A nucleus is the most important little organ or "organelle" inside a Eukaryotic cell – it's like the control tower of the cell. The nucleus is as important to a cell as is a brain to a human body.

Just like a cell has
- a **membrane**
- a jelly-like fluid called **cytoplasm** and
- a central **nucleus**,

the nucleus *also has*
- a **membrane**
- a jelly-like fluid called
  nucleoplasm (*nu-cleo-pla-sm*) and
- a densely compacted center
  called **nucleolus** (*nu-cle-o-lus*).

Let's take a closer look at each of these.

Nuclear membrane: The nucleus is bound by its own "skin" which separates the nucleus from the cell's cytoplasm. Inside this membrane, it contains the majority of the cell's genetic material.
It's actually a double membrane, an outer membrane and an inner

5 The Nucleus

Membrane. The outer membrane is surrounded by cytoplasm. The inner membrane does not come in contact with cytoplasm but it encloses fluid inside the nucleus, the nucleoplasm. You can think of it like a football which has an outer surface and an inner surface.

The cell needs to transfer material in and out of the nucleus. This happens via nuclear pore like structures in the membrane. But it's not a simple hole. As you can imagine, if you were to punch a hole in the football, all the air will just come out. Similarly, the nuclear pore is a special complex which allows only special particles to go in and out of the nucleus.

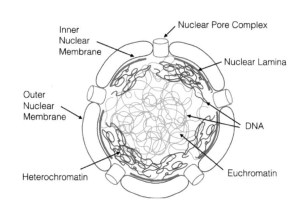

Nucleolus: The dense material inside the nucleus is the nucleolus - packed with the *DNA* of the cell. DNA has the information that directs the cell on what its structure needs to be and what operation it needs to perform. The DNA in the cells of an animal, for example, defines color of its eyes, the type of skin, the type of hair it might have, its height and weight, its eating preferences, living environment, etc.

For example, the reason a **hedgehog** has spines is because its DNA is programmed to have hollow hair which is made stiff with a substance called keratin.

Similarly, incase of a **bald eagle**, it defines the color and shape of its beak and feathers, the shape and functioning of its claws etc.

6 Deoxy-Ribo What?

6 Deoxy-Ribo What?

Deoxyribonucleic (*Dee-oxi-rybo-noo-cle-ic*) acid or DNA for short.

DNA is to living things like **recipe** is to food.

DNA is the genetic material that provides the blueprint for all living things. It gets passed from parents to child. From the color of a child's eyes and their physical appearance to their preferences, tastes, likes, dislikes etc, everything is determined by DNA.

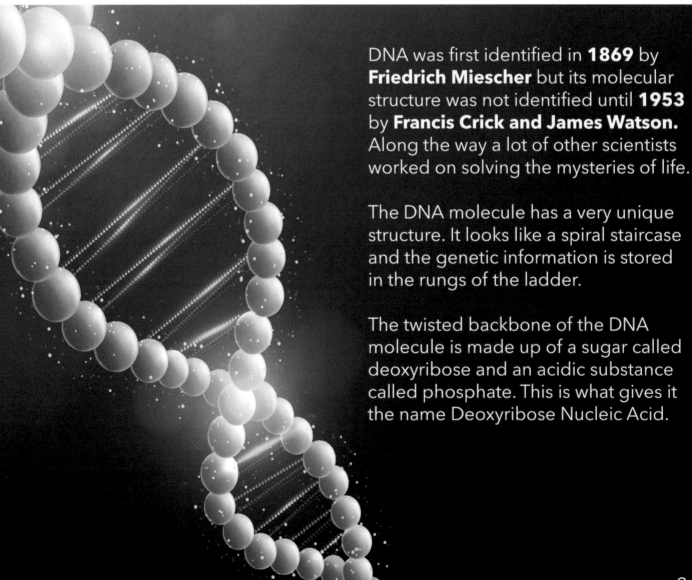

DNA was first identified in **1869** by **Friedrich Miescher** but its molecular structure was not identified until **1953** by **Francis Crick and James Watson.** Along the way a lot of other scientists worked on solving the mysteries of life.

The DNA molecule has a very unique structure. It looks like a spiral staircase and the genetic information is stored in the rungs of the ladder.

The twisted backbone of the DNA molecule is made up of a sugar called deoxyribose and an acidic substance called phosphate. This is what gives it the name Deoxyribose Nucleic Acid.

6 Deoxy-Ribo What?

Each rung is made up of a pair of substances called bases. There are 4 types of bases:

Adenine (A), Thymine (T), Cytosine (C) and **Guanine (G)**

A always pairs with T while C always pairs with G.

I like to think of them as 4 kids where A & T are best friends and C and G are best friends and are inseparable.

Genes are strings of these four bases, for example TTAC might be a gene sequence.

You can think of these sequences as **short words** which **combine to form sentences** which carry the code that defines all the features and characteristics of that living thing such as the color of their eyes.

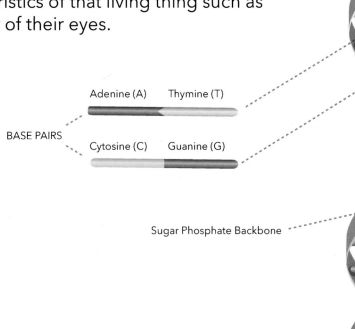

Adenine (A)   Thymine (T)

BASE PAIRS

Cytosine (C)   Guanine (G)

Sugar Phosphate Backbone

6 Deoxy-Ribo What?

A child might look similar to her mom because the information coded in her genes that define her face might be very similar to the information coded in her mom's genes that define her face. Similarly, the child's DNA sequence would be very different than the DNA sequence carried inside the cells of another species such as a bird. Each species passes on a lot of its genetic information to its future generations and hence the members of a species tend to have a lot of similarities.

All the genetic information is stored in these base pairs. The DNA lives inside a structure called a Chromosome (kro-mo-so-m). The chromosome looks like a "X" and the DNA is tightly coiled inside it.

If we look at the human body, has over **6,000,000,000,000 (6 Billion) base pairs**. The amazing thing is that all those 6 Billion pairs in the DNA are stored in just 23 pairs of chromosomes (or 46 chromosomes). Each parent contributes one of each pair of chromosomes in the baby.

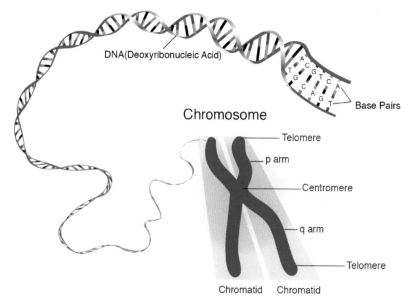

Courtesy: National Human Genome Research Institute

As shown in this picture, the X shaped chromosomes have a tightly-coiled strand of DNA, which have the sequences of base pairs, which contain the

6 Deoxy-Ribo What?

information about the genetic features of a living thing.

So to recap, the human body has trillions of cells. Each cell has a nucleus. The nucleus has 23 pairs of chromosomes and the chromosomes have DNA strands which have over 6 Billion base pairs and all the information about the human body resides in these base pairs.

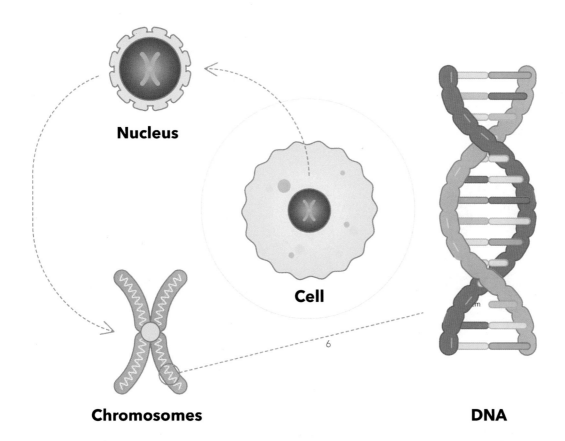

Nucleus

Cell

Chromosomes

DNA

Fun Fact
Even though we are all made of the same 4 base pairs A, T, C & G, the DNA in each and every human being is unique and can be used to identify an individual - so much so - that it is used by police to solve criminal cases by matching the DNA found at the site of the crime to the DNA of the suspects.

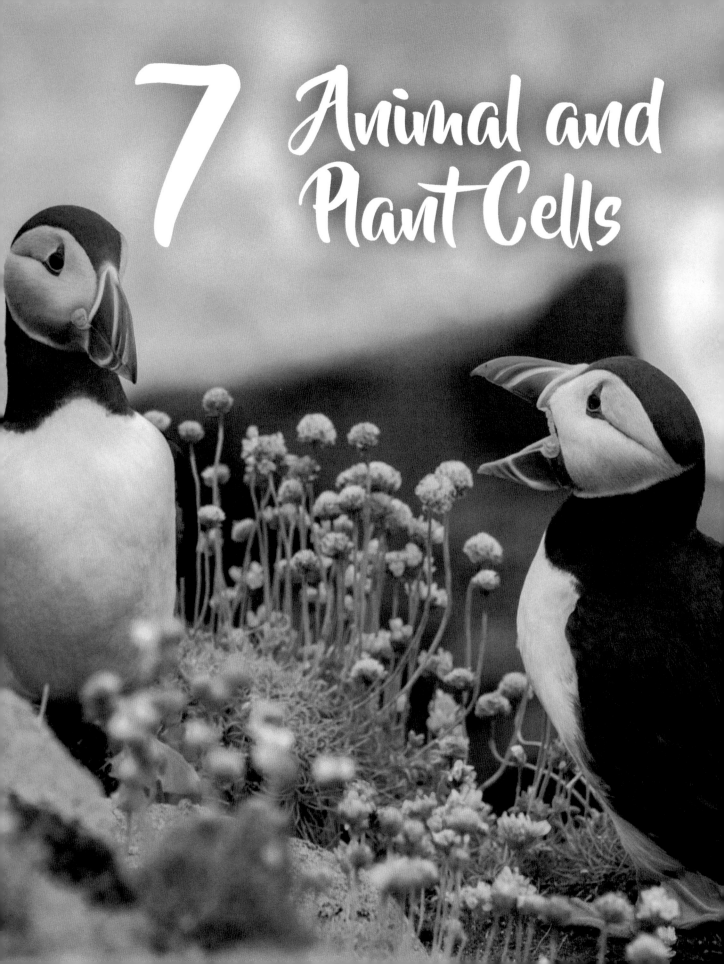

7 Animal and Plant Cells

7 Animal and Plant Cells

Let's learn a little bit more about plant and animal cells.

Plants and animals are made of **Eukaryotic** cells that are specialized to perform certain functions.

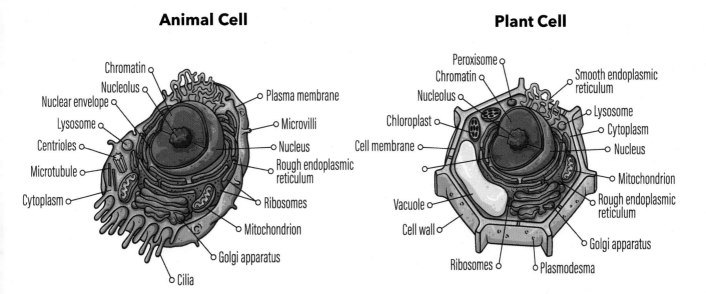

As we learnt earlier, both these types of cells have a nucleus which contains DNA, a membrane and cytoplasm. Since both animal and plant cells are eukaryotic, they have more similarities between each other. They both have similar processes for reproduction and similar processes for obtaining energy needed to grow. They also have similar cell structures called organelles that perform specialized operation needed for the workings of the cell.

Despite all these similarities the 2 types of cells are very different and perform many different functions. One of the biggest differences is that **plants absorb carbon-di-oxide from the atmosphere and convert it into oxygen** before releasing it back into the atmosphere. This process is called **photosynthesis** (*photo-syn-th-e-sys*).
Animals, on the **contrary, consume this oxygen from the atmosphere**

and convert it into carbon-di-oxide before it breathing it out. This is the process of respiration or breathing.

Without plants, the earth would not have any oxygen and animals would not be able to survive. Let's try to learn more about animal and plant cells by understanding one operation that each of these cells can perform.

What is Photosynthesis - *In case you are starting to imagine that plants know how to take selfies,* let me stop you. **"Photo"** means "Light" and **"synthesis"** means "to put together". Photosynthesis is a process where plants absorb the light coming from the sun, water & nutrients from the soil, and carbon-di-oxide from the atmosphere and convert it into food. In the process, oxygen is also generated as a by-product which the plants release back into the atmosphere.

Sunlight + Carbon-di-oxide = Food + Oxygen

Photosynthesis

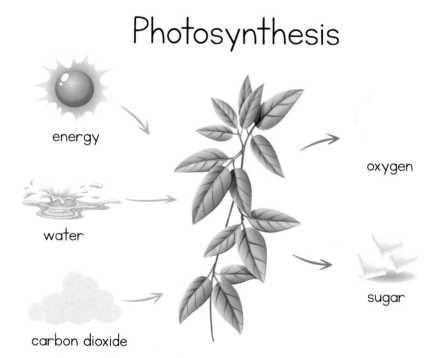

energy

water

carbon dioxide

oxygen

sugar

This is awesome for us humans because we need both oxygen and food to survive.

For this to happen, plants have some special components called **chloroplasts** (*klo-ro-plasts*) which contain a green pigment called **chlorophyll** (*klo-ro-fill*). This is why plants are **green** in color.

Now let's turn our attention to animals. To understand how tiny little cells make up an animal, let's take an example of a car.

Just like a car is made up of many different components such as an ***engine, ignition, steering wheel, brakes, tires, seats, transmission system*** etc. The car works when the ignition turns on the engine, the steering wheel directs the wheels in the right direction and the engine powers the transmission system, to move the car. All these different components work together to make the car work.

Similarly, the human (or animal) body is made up of different cells such as ***stem cells, blood cells, nerve cells, bone cells,*** etc. Each of these cell types performs a very specific function. For example, blood cells have the very important task of carrying oxygen from the lungs to all the different parts of the body that need oxygen. Similarly, nerve cells transmit information throughout the body in the form of electrical signals or nerve impulses so when your brain tells your hand to grab that apple, the information is being transmitted via the nerve cells in the body.

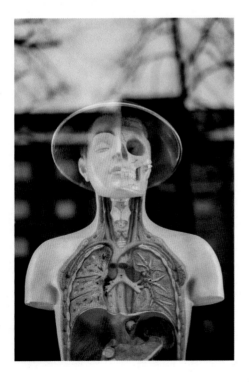

All these cells work together to make the operation of a human body possible. In this section we will learn a little bit more about red blood cells.

When you breathe in, you take oxygen from the atmosphere into the lung s. From the lungs this oxygen needs to be transported to all parts of the body, heart, brain, arms and all the way down to your toes. When you breathe out, all the carbon-di-oxide needs to be expelled from the body back out into the atmosphere. This is the job of Red Blood Cells. These cells are red because of a molecule called haemoglobin (he-mo-glo-bin). The oxygen in the air binds itself to this molecule which makes it possible to transport it.

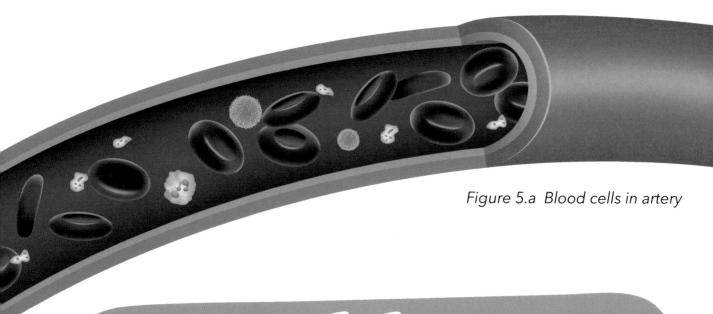

Figure 5.a Blood cells in artery

Fun Fact

Red Blood Cells, also known as RBCs, are shaped like donuts and are very flexible because they often need to be squeeze through thin blood capillaries without getting stuck. People with heart diseases have problems because their arteries become clogged and the blood cells have trouble getting through them. If the other parts of the body do not get the right amount of oxygen on time, they start dying so RBCs have a very important job.

About the Author

Garima lives with her husband and 10 year old son in the Silicon Valley. Garima has a Masters in Telecommunication and Software Engineering and a Bachelors Engineering Degree in Computer Engineering. The idea of this book is a marriage between her love of biology, books and the desire to spend quality time with her son.

About the Illustrator

Michael Lu and his wife lives in sunny Sri Lanka, and works as a full time user interface engineer and graphic designer with clients around the world. He enjoys working on creating delight in all of his work. In his spare time you will often find him playing with his 15 cats, four rabbits and also riding his pet unicorn.

Note to Parents

Dear Parents,

This brings us to the end of the first book in a series. We hope you and your child have enjoyed reading it and learnt about living and nonliving things. We also hope to continue adding more books to this series with more details on each topic and also introductions to more topics such as physics, chemistry, python *(programming languge),* Computers & Machine learning

If you have any feedback for us to make these books better, please feel free to reach out to us at
simplebooks4kids@gmail.com

We look forward to hearing from you.
Happy reading!

Photo Credits

Hummingbird: Photo by Zdeněk Macháček on Unsplash (Page
Panther: Photo by Uriel Soberanes on Unsplash
Dolphin: Photo by Louan García on Unsplash
Pebbles: Photo by Oliver Paaske on Unsplash
Penguins: Photo by Paul Carroll on Unsplash
Squirrel: Photo by Caleb Martin on Unsplash
Tulips: Photo by John-Mark Smith on Unsplash
Cactus: Photo by Alex Furgiuele on Unsplash
Lone Tree: Photo by Todd Quackenbush on Unsplash
Mom and baby Zebras: Photo by Vincent van Zalinge on Unsplash
Blue Whale: Photo by Vincent van Zalinge on Unsplash
Jelly Fish: Photo by Karan Karnik on Unsplash
Giraffes: Photo by sutirta budiman on Unsplash
Zebras: Photo by sutirta budiman on Unsplash
Tall trees in a forest: Photo by Luke Stackpoole on Unsplash
Moss: Photo by Markus Spiske on Unsplash
Lone Cactus: Photo by Karl Magnuson on Unsplash
People on a busy street: Photo by Artur Kraft on Unsplash
Hedgehog: Photo by Tadeusz Lakota on Unsplash
Bald Eagle: Photo by Mathew Schwartz on Unsplash
Puffins: Photo by Wynand van Poortvliet on Unsplash
Human Anatomy: Photo by Samuel Zeller on Unsplash
Car: Photo by Alwin Kroon on Unsplash

Made in the
USA
Columbia, SC